A Higher Calling

Homeschooling High School for Harried Husbands

Matt Binz,
Mr. HomeScholar

First Printing, 2016

Printed in the United States of America
Cover Design by Robin Montoya
Edited by Kimberly Charron

ISBN: 1511452846
ISBN-13: 978-1511452847

A Higher Calling

Homeschooling High School
for Harried Husbands

What are Coffee Break Books?

A Higher Calling is part of The HomeScholar's Coffee Break Book series.

Designed especially for parents who don't want to spend hours and hours reading a 400-page book on homeschooling high school, each book combines Lee's practical and friendly approach with detailed, but easy-to-digest information, perfect to read over a cup of coffee at your favorite coffee shop!

Never overwhelming, always accessible and manageable, each book in the series will give parents the tools they need to tackle the tasks of homeschooling high school, one warm sip at a time.

Everything about these Coffee Break Books is designed to connote simplicity, ease, and comfort - from the size (fits in a purse), to the font and paragraph length (easy on the eyes), to the price (the same as a Starbucks Venti Triple Caramel Macchiato). Unlike a fancy coffee drink, however, these books are guilt-free pleasures you will want to enjoy again and again!

Table of Contents

Introduction

"No Duh" Observations from an Amateur Dad

I realize that eight years as a homeschooling dad does not make me an expert. Factor in that I spent most of that time at my day job and you can rightfully conclude that I never made it out of the homeschooling farm league (A-ball ... nowhere near "The Show").

I did, however, get to do a lot of observing, both of my family and the broader educational system in America. My tenth grade English teacher, Mr. Oldenburger, tried to pummel into me, "The most important step to good compare and contrast writing is to stop and observe." I did a lot of that. Partly because I was baffled and partly because my wife, Lee (aka The HomeScholar) was and is a homeschooling force of nature. She tackled homeschooling with the commitment and intensity normally reserved for North Korean news anchors.

Unlike these sad and humorless minions, however, Lee is great at observing and pointing out the frailties of our educational system (both the bureaucratic train wreck we pass off as public education, and our own humble homeschool), and is better known in our family as "Our Lady of Perpetual Whining."

Most of what I reflect on in this book was borne from long conversations with Lee, typically after the kids fell asleep (sometime in 2006). My goal is to help homeschool dads understand and appreciate the noble endeavor they are engaged in and to encourage them to take their role seriously, and for heaven's sake, do more than yell at the kids to go to bed (spoiler alert ... that never works).

Finally, I want to remind dads that homeschooling is not a guarantee of future success or a panacea for life's problems. Homeschooling is much more like baking a soufflé than it is like car repair. It is not simply a matter of the right diagnosis, the right parts, and the right tools. It's more like throwing together a bunch of ingredients and hoping what comes out is edible. You can probably guess by my sophisticated description of car repair and soufflé baking, that I am lousy at both. But in life, as in cooking, sometimes the soufflé falls. You can't control it, all you can do is scrape it out, soak the pan, and try again. And to water board the metaphor further ... don't beat yourself up (or be overly proud) of the end results. Children, like soufflés, sometimes fall. You are responsible to do your best, get help when needed, and keep praying.

If you enjoy this book, please write a review on Amazon. My wife will carefully filter them so as to protect my delicate self-esteem. I am, after all, the product of a public school education.

Part One:

The Twit Olympics

(OR Why it isn't Hard to Beat a Public School Education)

Chapter 1

The Impossible Dream

Imagine you are a public school teacher on the first day of class, faced with 30 children, none of whom speak English. Worse yet, imagine there are 10 unique languages spoken by the students, with no language spoken by more than five students. How would you communicate? How would you teach?

More importantly, how would anyone learn?

You might think this illustration absurd, but consider the differences in your own children. Our two boys are built so differently that Lee and I often wondered if one or possibly both of them were switched at birth. Everything about how they view life, friendships, work, and academics is different. Yet these two share the same DNA, parents, and upbringing.

Now ask yourself—wouldn't teaching 30 utterly unique souls be somewhat akin to teaching in our imaginary multi-lingual classroom? In addition to the normal crowd control, behavior modification, and refereeing, we would need to somehow unlock the mystery of communication and inspiration in each child.

Speaking their Language

I believe this works best when a child sits at the feet of someone who "speaks their language," someone who has a deep love and commitment to their well-being.

Who do you think is more qualified than you to provide this environment?

My boss was bemoaning the fact that his precious pet, a two-year-old Bernese Mountain Dog, had suddenly acquired a taste for leather shoes and iPhones. And by "acquired a taste," I mean in the most literal sense of the expression.

I asked him about obedience training and he said the dog was in obedience training three times a week and was doing great! The trainer apparently spoke fluent Bernese. My boss, however ... not so much. As a result, all that great education was left in the classroom when his baby came home and got a whiff of the latest luxury item.

The point is that living things are not computer code, and education is more than pouring information in. Success requires tremendous care and attention. Don't believe anyone who tells you homeschooling is easy. They are either deluded or selling you something. Homeschooling is hard, like parenting is hard.

But homeschooling is important—as important as parenting. Don't ever think you will be successful simply because you are so very clever or well educated. Ultimately, success will come because you love and understand your children enough to "speak their language."

And that is the secret of parenting, homeschooling, and dog training.

Chapter 2

An Educational Tragedy of the Commons

There was big news recently for Seattle public high schools. After a long hiatus, the "E" is back.

And what, you ask, is the "E"?

"E" is the socially acceptable designator to signify a failing grade. It was apparently decided that giving an "F" was much too damaging for a failing student's self-esteem.

Alas, even moving from "Flunk" to the more values-neutral "Eww" was a little too harsh for the delicate sensibilities of our feel-good generation.

So in 2000, those nasty F's and E's were replaced by the even more ambiguous "N," which stands for "No Credit." Getting an "N" in a class is the academic equivalent of winning the immunity idol on the TV show, Survivor. An individual's poor performance is "Neutralized" by a grade that does not get credited to their GPA.

Thus, with a bit of planning, a student could theoretically fail Math, Science, English, and History, get an "A" in P.E., and emerge from the semester victorious with a 4.0 GPA!

After years of hyperventilating while inflating grades, woozy district leaders caught their breath long enough to issue a resolution declaring this situation to be "bad." (Perhaps "not optimal" would be less harsh.)

And we wonder why our schools are failing! In the scientific realm, we believe in Newton's Third Law of Motion ("for every action, there is an equal and opposite reaction"), but in the educational realm we deny it.

In our public high schools, students can embark on a four year adventure in mediocrity and be propped up by a system that is resolute in its denial of failure. My guess is that students from such high schools will fully experience Newton's promised "equal and opposite reaction" about a day after entering the job market, where failure is always an option.

You see, in the real world, Newton's Law is enforced by Darwin's Law, "survival of the fittest."

But why do some leaders fail to understand that natural consequences are, in fact, natural? Why can't they see that in the normal course of events, some students will succeed and others will fail? Why won't they acknowledge that emphasizing good feelings does much more harm to failing students than allowing them to experience a little reality based therapy?

Traditional answers to this question are often framed around self-esteem arguments. Specifically, a person who feels good about themselves will eventually seek to become the person they believe they truly are. But by emphasizing their inherent goodness, failing students are protected from the one reality check that might open their eyes to their true situation.

Despite plenty of evidence to the contrary, I believe what our educational leaders lack is *not* common sense (work with me here).

I believe what they lack is ownership.

Our children are caught in a system that is designed for throughput rather than education. Think about the normal progression of events from the time your precious child enters the public school system.

First, there is half day kindergarten, followed by half day daycare. Here, Junior is conditioned to behave in a way that will minimize disruption.

"Getting along" is the chief civic virtue.

For the next six years, Junior is passed along annually to a new teacher who becomes the custodian responsible for managing his behavior and, hopefully, teaching him a thing or two. Each year, Junior must learn to deal with a new educational custodian.

When Junior becomes unbearable for a single adult to deal with for a full day (generally around seventh grade), the burden is broken into more manageable 50 minute segments, also known as class periods. Ownership of his education becomes even more diffused.

After nine months of learning to deal with multiple custodians with multiple sets of expectations, Junior and his entire grade are packaged and shipped downstream to the next group of unsuspecting educators. Heaven forbid any student should fail! This would mean that teachers would need to endure them for an additional year!

If he doesn't drop out, Junior will graduate having achieved, on average, one of the lowest levels of academic preparation in any industrialized nation.

You get the picture. The process starts when a child steps on the public school stage and is perpetuated and reinforced by each actor in the play. No one in this sorry chain of events ever takes real ownership of the child's education!

I believe we are experiencing a cultural "tragedy of the commons." When something is owned "in common," few, if any, will be fully committed to protect and nurture it. This happens in our world all the time—from African wildlife reserves to inner city parks. When the ownership of something is unclear, people feel less constrained about misusing or exploiting it. Vacant buildings attract graffiti vandals like curriculum sales attract homeschool moms!

Ownership, however, promotes responsibility and constrains exploitation.

So, how can we use this insight to address our very real "Tragedy of the

Educational Commons?" First, we need to begin promoting ownership in education. But, if not the government, who should own our children's education?

Parents!

Parents *know* their children and *love* their children—something that is impossible for the state to replicate.

Care is a lousy substitute for love. Children know and respond to those who love them, but they can smell phony "care" a mile off. I sometimes wonder if the onset of "normal teenage rebellion" might mark the time when kids finally get fed up with adult "care."

Kids deserve the commitment of parents, not only the care of the state. I believe all children have a natural hunger to learn that can be suppressed by systemic neglect. Some kids find the connections they need to thrive in our public schools. Far too many, however, get lost in a system designed to deal with groups rather than individuals. Children and parents alike are tuned in enough to know intuitively that something is amiss in our schools.

But reform moves in geological time while children grow at light speed. Parents, recognizing the system won't change in time to benefit their own children, are left with a choice. Do they sacrifice their kids to what they know is a failed system, or do they take on ownership of their kids' education through homeschooling?

Homeschooling parents reject passivity and assertively take ownership of their children's education. They protect their children from negative societal influence and place them in an environment where they can thrive.

They cherish, they challenge, they correct, but most of all, they love.

They do all this because they want their children, as unique creations of God, to get an education perfectly suited for their needs.

It isn't a guarantee of success, but it is the best chance you have.

Chapter 3

The High Cost of Improving Public Schools

It is amazing what you can find on public access TV on a lazy Saturday morning. For no apparent reason, I watched a Department of Education panel discussion featuring representatives of several charter schools in New Jersey. One school, with a waiting list of 1500 families, featured an extended school day (7:30 AM - 5:30 PM), an extended school week (every other Saturday), an extended school year (mid-August through the end of June), and truckloads of extended homework. A panelist boasted that this allowed the students to get "50% more educational time" than other public school students. The results? Average test scores went from the 15th percentile to the 75th percentile in four years.

Impressive? Absolutely, but at what cost?

Fifty percent more educational time can also be translated as 50% less time with the family. For younger kids, it also means 50% less time playing with friends, 50% less time for delight-directed learning, and 50% less time getting to know grandparents. For older students, it can mean 50% less time developing their area of passion, 50% less time giving back to the community through church or public service, and 50% less time for meaningful employment.

Are the results worth it? I suppose it depends on your perspective. If your goal is higher test scores regardless of the collateral damage, then by all means, yes. If your goal is growing educated citizens, while at the same time building strong, cross-generational relationships, you might want to consider other options.

Homeschooling, whether classical, eclectic, or unschooling, is a profoundly efficient way to educate children. We can also gain that "extra FLAV-R boost" of an education while still providing time for other important aspects of growing up. Do we really need to sacrifice childhood, family, faith, and friends on the altar of education?

No! Education is extremely important, but it is not the *most* important. Parents must keep a firm grasp on their ultimate goal and not accept the fashionable belief that a quality education is only possible by spending exorbitant amounts of time in a classroom.

But what makes homeschooling so efficient? I believe it is because of two fundamental factors: the teachers and the learning environment.

First, homeschooling is education delivered by people who know their children deeply, love them profoundly, and are committed to them unconditionally. In addition, homeschooling is education delivered in a secure environment, absolutely devoid of harassment and intimidation. Taken together, these two factors have the same effect on children as taking a regulator out of a high performance race car. We were amazed at the amount and speed at which our children learned when we started homeschooling.

Those of us who "tasted" public school before beginning to homeschool know this perhaps better than those who have homeschooled their children from the start.

The massive waiting list typical of charter schools indicates a profound hunger in society for improving the ways we educate our children. If we are seeking alternatives to what the current system offers, we need only to turn our hearts toward home. Homeschooling through high school builds strong, confident, and educated citizens while strengthening vital relationships that will last a lifetime.

And you can do it in 50% less time, with 100% less anxiety, and 1000% more confidence!

Part Two:

Working Together

(OR Why a Three Stranded Cord is Better for Tying Up the Kids)

Matt Binz, Mr. HomeScholar

Chapter 4

Homeschooling Revolutionaries

Homeschoolers are a rebellious bunch. Their lives are filled with everyday insurrections and ten-cent treasons. You know who you are.

- Moms who sign their declaration of intent with the same spirit that John Hancock signed the Declaration of Independence (*shock!*)
- Dads who alarm their friends and neighbors by educating their kids during the summer (*shudder!*)
- Students who "stick it to the man" by forgoing prom (*tremble!*)

In general, you firebrands demonstrate a wanton disregard for societal norms by taking personal responsibility for your children's education. (*gasp!*)

But revolution is tiring business. I've noticed a trend in families - they lose their subversive tendencies as their students approach high school. After pulling up roots from the old country and staking their claim in the new world, many lose their rebel vision.

It seems they forget the reasons for rebelling.

Homeschool fatigue is entirely understandable. When friends, family and "the system" stand in judgment of you 24/7, it is enough to make your knees shake.

Doubts creep in: "Maybe they're right ... maybe we are ruining our children ... maybe we are destroying their future."

Gradually, the features of traditional education that used to send you into a seditious froth begin to look more attractive. (Well, if not attractive, at least less revolting.) After all, a classroom setting offers tradition, security, a built-in social network, and free curriculum. In essence, the world is tempting you with a ready-made answer to all your high school fears.

At this stage, parents resemble the children of Israel who looked back at Egypt and longed for what had driven them away!

"4b) Who will give us curriculum to use?
5) We remember the stuff we used to get free in the Public Schools, the math, and the science, and the reading, and the social studies.
6) But now our desire is gone. There is nothing at all to look at except for this pile of bills."
(Numbers 11: 4b-6, New Homeschool Version)

Like the children of Israel, such homeschool families face a crossroads. Which path will they choose: the one-size-fits-all "solutions" offered by traditional schools, or the road less traveled into homeschooling high school?

Fathers play a critical role at this crossroad. Oftentimes, homeschool moms are so enmeshed in the daily grind of lesson plans, schedules, and keeping the house that they can't see the forest for the trees. Dads are needed to help draw the family back to the reasons why they chose to set sail to this new world in the first place.

"Without a Vision, the people perish."
(Proverbs 29: 18)

Dads are called to be the guardians and vision keepers. They need to be prepared when the king's forces come back to lay claim to what they consider their rightful property. Sometimes the king will launch a frontal attack - for example, legislative action to outlaw homeschooling. But more often, the assaults are subtle: a sideways remark about socialization, a parent who sadly comments on your child missing the prom, a friend who shares their concern about whether your child will make it into college.

These attacks are real, and the truth is, they can hurt.

After hearing such whispers for years, it is common for even the bravest homeschool parent to crack. One such mom confessed to us during a recent homeschool convention that she was going to put her child back in public high school next fall. When asked why, she couldn't give a reasonable response.

It was obvious that she was flat out tired - weary of defending herself to friends and family. She doubted whether homeschooling would work anymore. We asked whether homeschooling was working so far. "Oh yes, it has been wonderful ..." she said, wistfully.

Following the time honored maxim "If it ain't broke ..." we suggested that perhaps high school would be a success as well. We gave her some hope and suggestions and she left, committed to pray about it more. Not insignificantly, she came to our booth alone. Her husband was not there to help her stand.

So, what can be done?

The solution is not too complicated. Men, you need to understand the pressures that are placed on your homeschooling wife. Even in a perfectly supportive environment, homeschooling high school is tough business. Add the persistent drip, drip, drip of society questioning her work and she can easily lose hope.

And when hope has waned, despair quickly fills the void.

One definition of a leader is a person who brokers hope. Husbands, step up and lead! Beat back the darkness! Remind your family about why you chose to homeschool. Talk about the homeschooling issues and develop a plan that you can implement together. Discuss the benefits you have already experienced through your homeschool and the benefits you expect in the future.

Above all, underscore your commitment to this path by sharing the household burden!

That's right ... sometimes the path from utter despair to renewed hope can be blocked by something as mundane as a sink full of dirty dishes!

Not to put too fine of a point on it, men, put down the remote and help!

Take responsibility for some of the housework! Teach your kids a subject! This means plan it, make the assignments, give the instruction, grade the papers, and give them feedback. In addition to lifting the burden on your wife, your kids will pick up on the not so subtle message that Dad is taking charge and they need to answer to him alone!

All homeschool families need to remember that there will always be a day of reckoning for revolutionaries. It's out there, so prepare!

Moms—lean on those who have gone before you and can offer hope.

Parents—talk to each other about roles and responsibilities. Remind and encourage each other about why you chose this path.

Dads—above all, take some of the load off your wife.

Husbands, the gallows of history are filled with solo revolutionaries! Hang together so your wife won't hang alone!

Chapter 5

The Economics of Fear

In our neighborhood there is a quaint relic of a bygone era known as 5-Corners. Sure, 5-Corners is an intersection, but it is also much more. In reality, it is a silent monument to the greater Seattle area's proud history of alcoholic traffic planners.

From 5-Corners, you are faced with a plethora of options. You can turn right, veer right, go straight, turn left, or assume the transportation equivalent of the lotus position, doubling back on yourself in a truly unnatural act of automotive contortion.

As I waited at the red light, weighing my options, I thought about the myriad of choices awaiting homeschool families as they enter the high school years. Far from only moving straight ahead, there are dozens of billboards enticing families to veer off into some sort of educational Promised Land.

Straight ahead is homeschooling high school with graduation, college, and career success clearly visible over the next rise.

To the right are alt-ed programs with their promise of free curriculum and state sanctioned education.

Veer right toward co-ops with their ready-made social structures and pre-chosen curriculum.

To the left are accreditation agencies and certified teachers who entice you with a "certified" transcript and "professional" educators.

Doubling back to the left will lead you to public schools but that road, I've heard, is filled with pot holes, nails, and broken dreams.

So, which way to choose? The brightly colored signs are all very tempting. I wonder what would happen if I turned in another direction ...

As I consider turning right onto Alt-Ed Avenue, I begin to ponder the wisdom of my then 11 year old economist son, Alex, who was the first to reveal the hidden mysteries of our state controlled economy to me.

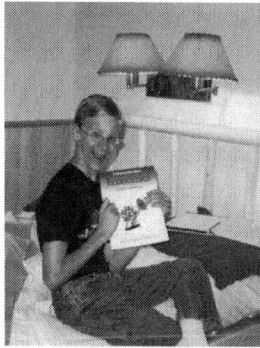

Alex, age 11, studies economics

"Dad," he said, stroking what in years to come would grow into thick blond stubble, "in a normal economic exchange, both parties are saying that they value the thing they gain more than the thing they give up. The problem with exchanges with the government is that you can never be really sure about what you are giving up."

"Not bad for a midget." I think, as I'm filled with a proud paternal glow.

In terms of alt-ed, what this means (I think) is that what you gain is tangible—money for books, curriculum, and lessons. What you give up is less obvious, but not less valuable. What value do you place on being able to educate your own children? How much money would you need in exchange for the right to freely communicate your faith and values to your kids? In truth, alt-ed is making the most craven of appeals: money in exchange for your children. Now, I'm sure I love a good red porridge as much as Esau did, but not nearly enough to sell my birthright.

Well then, how about veering off onto Co-op Court? What could possibly be wrong with teaming up with like-minded homeschool moms in order to educate your kids? Seems perfectly harmless, right? Perhaps. But again, the annoyingly high pitched memory of my pre-adolescent son's voice comes to me:

"Dad, what will you be giving up? Is it worth less than what you gain?"

Alex, age 75, Federal Reserve Chairman (age enhanced photo)

In the case of co-ops, what you give up is control. Not control in a bad sense, but in the positive sense of homeschooling independently:

- The ability to choose the perfect curriculum for your child, one that is tailor fit for their needs and passions.
- Control of the speed at which you move through the school year, with the ability to start, stop, and

rearrange to perfectly meet the needs of your child and family.

- Control to allow a true measure of delight-directed learning along with the more standard curriculum.
- And, perhaps most importantly, control to guide your child toward healthy relationships in the broader context of society, rather than giving them over to the frequently shallow attachments common in any classroom setting.

Many co-ops started out as small bands of moms, but have grown so large and structured that it is virtually impossible to distinguish them from public schools. One co-op board member complained that a student came rushing through the hallways and around the corner, smacking right into her. To his credit, the student apologized before dashing off. What was significant about this event was that our friend confessed she didn't have a clue who the child was.

Think about that. A co-op leader who had been involved in the founding of the co-op did not recognize one of the students! We were surprised until we learned that this particular co-op had over a thousand students! Nobody could keep track of that many kids!

OK, but how about Accreditation Lane by way of Certification Circle? Surely, if you want to get to college, you need to travel there. That has a *lot* of value, right? Once again, my young Milton Friedman comes to me ...

"Dad, you know the oldest trick in the book is to try destroying the value of what the other person has in order to convince them that exchanging with you is in their best interest. Think about why you bought your Wii. Wasn't it because you were convinced your PlayStation 2 wasn't cool enough? And now, they both sit there, silently mocking you ..."

At this point, I'm tempted to throw my nunchuk at him but remember I'm in my car, not playing my beloved, but somewhat dusty, Wii.

With accreditation agencies, you give up autonomy and control to gain a piece of paper that declares your homeschool "accredited" and your report card "official." Never mind that most colleges don't care much about accreditation or "official grades," or that even some public high schools aren't accredited. So how do these groups convince so many to take this left turn?

They use fear.

They reinforce your doubts by suggesting that you are incapable or will fail your children if you teach them independently. They raise the stakes by reminding you how much you can lose if you don't homeschool "correctly." They make homeschooling high school seem so difficult that no one could possibly do it without their help. You've got to give them credit - these are some powerful buttons they are pushing! Don't believe them for a second, though. It's a lie.

You *can* do it, and I can prove it. We did it ourselves!

So, what to do? Time is running out. It's time to choose!

The light turns green and I head straight...

Straight back home.

Chapter 6

The Seasons of Homeschooling

Caretaker, Teacher, Parent, Friend

Homeschool parents assume four primary roles throughout their children's lives: caretaker, teacher, mentor, and friend. These four roles are not unique to homeschool parents, although they seem to be more intense than they are for parents who have outsourced much of their children's education. Homeschool parents know, probably better than most, the exceedingly high stakes involved in educating their kids. If they fail, there is no external safety net. I believe an appreciation of this concept affects how homeschool parents approach all four roles, or seasons, of homeschooling.

Like the changing seasons in my hometown Seattle, these homeschooling seasons have no clearly defined start and stop. Parents play a caretaking role throughout their kids' childhoods. It is a role that gradually lessens over time (although the period of caretaking in the teenage years is probably as intense as any other time in a child's life). Parents who are committed to homeschooling their children do not have the luxury of anticipating a long stretch of childhood when the primary role of teacher will be delegated to others. The difference in attitude this makes is as subtle as it is important. A rough analogy is the changing attitudes humans have towards the environment over time.

When we first gathered into villages, our ancestors must have had a dawning realization that merely moving human waste outside the community's boundaries was a losing proposition. As time went on, I'm sure they concluded the mess would eventually need to be dealt with. Likewise, parents who shove their kids' educations "outside the gates" may think they have addressed their responsibilities, but may wonder why "the mess" keeps coming back to them.

The Responsible Teacher

Because they know they will be living with what they create, homeschool parents tend to be a bit more thoughtful in the execution of these four roles. Sure, it may be the instincts of a loving parent, but if we are honest with ourselves, there is also an element of self-preservation involved. "Hmm ... if I let little Timmy get away with being disrespectful today, how will that affect our lives with him tomorrow?" This is an important question that is not easily dismissed when Timmy is planted in our living room for the next 16 years.

Likewise, some parents who assume a supporting role in their children's education may adopt a defeatist attitude when dealing with behavioral problems. "Can you believe what they are teaching them in the schools?! What is this world coming to?!" Homeschool parents, however, recognize that success depends on their commitment and their ability to marshal the appropriate resources to support a productive learning environment.

Teen Truth or Consequences

Because the teaching role in a homeschool family is supercharged, the transition from teacher to mentor can be exceedingly challenging. The question is how do you move from being the one from whom all educational decisions flow (teacher role) to the one who must stand by and allow natural consequences to take their course (mentor role).

Well … sometimes the answer is poorly.

In our home, it took a while for us to come to grips with this shift. Being a homeschool teacher was—for the most part—a delightful family time. There is a bit of denial, however, when one considers that your children won't be homeschooling forever. This is why you never hear a homeschool mom say to her adult child, "Please don't schedule a late teleconference, sweetheart, you and I are doing a unit study on toads tonight."

This is a good thing, I suppose. Mom and Dad have earned the right to snicker at their own children's struggles as they homeschool their kids. But the transition can be difficult.

It is difficult because homeschool parents have spent years ensuring they cover everything. They've been vigilant not to leave gaps in their children's education. They've invested heavily in their children's areas of interest. They've spent sleepless nights praying for their spiritual journey. And then ... everything changes.

Kids start to grow up. They start the long and often painful transition from childhood to adulthood and begin to stretch their wings. This would be a universally joyous event except for one small problem.

They frequently screw it up.

That's right. They make mistakes. Shocking, frequent, painful mistakes. Mistakes that surely you never made (oftentimes true because you made your own shocking, frequent, and painful mistakes). Mistakes that can cost them and you dearly. And in this situation, what is the vigilant, supportive, hyper-competent homeschool parent supposed to do ...?

That's right—let them fail!

Letting Go - Again

Ugh! This was the part I hated most about homeschooling. It got to the point where it wasn't enough to bite my tongue; I needed to sew my lips shut. I became one of those parents who went around muttering to myself, "I'll teach him what it means to work hard ... doesn't he understand what he's doing?" Because I would usually be looking down as I muttered, I'm sure the dog was convinced he was going to get kicked.

But a funny thing happened. After a while, they started to learn! I remember when my eldest was 10 months old, Lee and I could sit and watch him for hours at the coffee table:

Standwobblecrashstandwobblecrash standwobblecrash ...

Adorable, right? I must say however, this same basic pattern isn't nearly as amusing when they are 19. "The bigger they are, the harder they fall," has never been truer.

In our house, what was true at 19 was utterly different at 20. In a year, our eldest went from ignoring everything we said to repeating everything we said. It's true. Often, after he visited from college we came away thinking we had a conversation with ourselves! It was miraculous. Something happened and he seemed to internalize nearly every parental lesson we had taught over the years (with the exception of hanging up his clothes - he obviously didn't get the memo).

Fatigue and Futility

On one hand, being a mentor to our adult children should be easy. They are adults and consequently get to make adult choices. What makes it hard is that as parents we still feel *so responsible*! You'd think all the years of being ignored would teach us we don't have control over our teens' choices. Intellectually, we get it. Emotionally, Lee and I were both 100% committed to pushing that rope, tied to that rock, up that hill.

Eventually, we didn't get smart, we simply got tired.

A funny thing happened when we let go. The kids seemed to sense we weren't protecting them as much and they started to behave more responsibly. Imagine that! I suppose after homeschooling them for so long, we should have known they weren't dumb. They started to get it.

So you see, the key to moving from teacher to mentor is to simply stop teaching so darn much. I'm serious!

You are not responsible for your adult child anymore. Let it go! If you are tempted to jump back in the middle of their lives, go find another distraction. Get a dog! You can train a dog and (if you are holding a treat) they will listen to you!

I don't want you to be discouraged, however. Mentors still get to teach. The key is that they get to teach only when asked. You are no longer a river of education flowing freely across the desert. No, you are a hose and you have a nozzle. Sometimes you may feel like an extremely high pressure hose, but you still need to be shut off until someone metaphorically squeezes your handle.

The Friendship Factor

The last season of homeschooling - which promises to last the longest - is the season of friendship. Finally, you and your kids are equals. You may find yourself learning as much or more from them as they do from you. You may seek their wisdom and counsel on problems you are having (it's technology issues for me).

There is freedom in simply being friends. The pressure is off and the relationship can find a center. I suppose the real payoff for all your hard work will come when they have kids of their own. You may then experience the delight of seeing your children on their own journey through the four seasons of homeschooling. If you are lucky, you will be asked to play an active role throughout. It doesn't get much better than that.

Part Three:

Dad Dreams

(OR Why Sometimes the Apple Rolls a Long Way from the Tree)

Chapter 7

The Homeschool High School Payoff

It was a wonderful week in Hawaii. Lee and I chaperoned our younger son, Alex, so he could chair a session and present his research to the Western Economics Association International Conference (WEAI) at the Sheraton in Waikiki! Despite the fact that Alex has traveled alone before and is comfortable in airports and hotels, we decided he *needed* an escort. It's a tough duty but sometimes we have to step up as parents.

This time we were smart, though. In the two previous years he presented to the

WEAI, we attended the conference. It was a huge mistake. Not only was it expensive, but neither Lee nor I understood what anyone was saying! This time we stayed away and enjoyed the beach and the sun. We did, however, watch Alex give his presentation. This time he had prepared us weeks in advance on his topic, so by the time we got there, we understood a little of what he was saying.

The presentation went very well, but the highlight for us came at the end when we overheard a conversation between Alex and one of the co-presenters. He was a professor from Bethany University that none of us knew, and Alex had met minutes before the presentation.

> **Professor**: Alex, how old are you, exactly?
> **Alex**: Eighteen
> **Professor**: So, you're obviously not a professor. Are you a graduate student?
> **Alex**: No, I'm a junior at Seattle Pacific University.

Professor (deep in thought): You were homeschooled, weren't you?

Think about that. Alex, who had been in a college setting for three years, was still identified as a homeschooler. This professor had seen enough homeschoolers to recognize the pattern—a young student operating with confidence in a gathering of economics professors and industry leaders, someone who was able to interact as a peer with professionals 20 to 50 years his senior. Someone with the passion to excel at a young age in the field he loves.

How cool is that?! An economics professor recognizes excellence in a young adult and attributes it to homeschooling!

In the broader community, homeschoolers are beginning to be noticed by adults. As I mention in my article on The HomeScholar website, "Don't Miss Manners," homeschool parents aren't the only ones playing the "spot the homeschooler" game. The popular misconception of antisocial homeschoolers unable to operate in society is being replaced with a more accurate picture of confident young men and women, who demonstrate passion and excellence.

I wonder how long my kids will be recognized as homeschoolers. As increasingly more kids graduate homeschool high school and move to college, my guess is this awareness will be more frequently articulated. Eventually, I predict the entire stereotype of the nerdy, shy homeschooler will be replaced by a much more accurate one, that of leader. As a side note, I sometimes wonder if the image of the shy and awkward homeschool student experiencing high school for the first time might be partly true. I know I'd be a bit shell-shocked if thrown into a comparably strange environment for the first time.

Say, for example, Mars.

Homeschoolers become leaders when they are given opportunities to lead at a young age. I have written before about how society's low expectations for teens can result in missed opportunities for our students to operate on a higher plane. This was not always the case. When our country was young, adolescents (a modern term) learned early on how to contribute and function in society. They gained a skill or trade by working alongside adults who acted as mentors.

Where does a young person in modern society get this sort of experience? They are in a classroom for six to eight hours a day where the student to teacher-mentor ratio is approximately 30:1. The lucky ones are then driven to extracurricular activities where the student to coach-mentor ratio is 20:1. Rarely do they get to have dinner with a parent-mentor. We should not be surprised that kids who socialize almost exclusively with other kids do not demonstrate adult skills or maturity.

Homeschooling high school places socialization in its natural form and proper context. Kids interact with all age groups in normal life situations. Before

Alex was able to present research at a professional conference, he spoke at length on economic issues with his grandfather and neighbor. My other son was a volunteer chess teacher for other homeschool children before he became a paid chess coach. These are the types of opportunities readily available to homeschooling families. Use them to set your student on the path toward excellence.

High school is the season in life when the benefits of homeschooling become evident to all. Some of our friends and family members were skeptical of homeschooling in the beginning. By the time children start high school, the social, moral, and academic preparation of homeschool students becomes difficult to deny. Colleges are certainly noticing and so are employers.

Excellence will always be rewarded in society. Christians expect it in their pastors. Citizens crave it in their politicians. Businesses demand it in their leaders. Homeschool high school graduates are in a unique position to fill these roles in society.

Not because they are better, but because they are better prepared.

Chapter 8

Blue Chip Teens

Do you ever wonder why seemingly rational institutions of higher learning yearly award millions of dollars of merit-based scholarships to pimply, wet-behind-the-ears teens?

When our 16 and 18 year old sons were awarded $184,000 in merit based scholarships to attend their first choice university, I have to admit that I did. Gazing into the train wreck that was their bedrooms, I asked myself, "What were they thinking?"

Here's a hint—universities don't grant merit scholarships out of a sense of duty or altruism.

It helps to remember that colleges are, first and foremost, businesses. They are making an investment. It is a gamble that in the future, these same confused, unkempt students will be the movers and shakers in society and will, in due time, shine a bright light back on the university from whose hallowed halls they emerged. Will they succeed and make the college proud? Will they go on to leadership positions in society? Will they ultimately earn enough money to leave an endowment? These questions play a significant, if perhaps subconscious, role in admission decisions.

As parents, you can use this insight to help your teens. Sometimes I think talking about marketing your teens to colleges sounds a bit craven. But if you think about it, marketing is simply the act of representing someone or something in the best possible light. It is what I do every morning when I ask my increasingly lonely hair to cover more and more forehead real estate.

College Admissions—A Jaded Bunch

As parents, we all think our children are gifted and talented. Homeschool parents—who typically have invested much of their adult lives actively helping their children to develop—may experience these feelings stronger than most. Unfortunately, college admissions officers are a fairly jaded bunch. They have seen *many* "gifted" teens cross their threshold and have learned how to quickly discern the hype from the real thing.

The first key to successfully marketing your teen to colleges is to ensure they are the "real thing." What I mean is, to design your homeschool so that in the end your child emerges educated, self-confident, wise (relatively speaking), self-motivated, and morally upright. Not an easy goal, to be sure, but one that homeschoolers seem to achieve more regularly than any other parent group in our society.

Parents do this because they are typically educated, self-confident, wise, motivated, and morally upright. A gross generalization, to be sure, but parents who aren't, tend to quickly drop out of homeschooling. Those who are left usually have the right stuff to guide and educate their children. In addition to these character traits, homeschool parents have the one other key ingredient that no school, from the worst inner-city institution to the most prestigious prep academy can replicate—that is, a true love for their children.

GILLIGAN!!!!

Homeschool parents deliver the goods. The question is how to demonstrate this best to colleges. The good news is that homeschooling is no longer a novelty. Colleges—even the most prestigious ones—have enough experience with homeschoolers that they no longer look at them as if fresh off Gilligan's Island.

This is good, because historically, the first step to gaining college acceptance is convincing them that homeschool kids are just like "normal kids." This might sound like a low standard but without early homeschool pioneers on college campuses, homeschool students might still be kept at arm's length—like the swine flu.

Without the fight to justify their normalcy, homeschool parents can focus on presenting their students' more refined characteristics. Here are a few key areas where parents can help their students communicate effectively during the college application process.

Academics

Lee and I often laugh about the "homeschool 4.0" —the default grade on many homeschool transcripts. But is there anything wrong with this strategy? Not as long as two conditions are met. The first is to structure your homeschool around the concept of mastery.

Our oldest son graduated from our homeschool high school with a perfect 4.0, even though he got a C in Algebra 1.

How can this be? Well, like many homeschool families, we looked at a C as unacceptable—an indication that mastery wasn't achieved—so we changed curriculum and tried again. With the right curriculum, Kevin found Algebra 1 a breeze and, consequently, earned his 4.0.

This is not unusual and represents one of the key strengths of homeschooling—the tendency of homeschool parents to demand mastery before moving on. One brief caveat—mastery is not the same as perfection. I have achieved mastery over addition and subtraction, but if you looked closely at my checkbook, you would quickly discover "imperfections." You can achieve mastery over concepts even if an occasional error is made.

The second condition of granting the homeschool 4.0 is to ensure you have some outside documentation supporting your assertion. This can come in the form of CLEP tests, SAT or ACT scores, community college grades, letters of recommendation from people outside the family, or even external evaluations.

Please remember, however, that you don't need to spend money on an outside accreditation agency to validate your homeschool. You can get this external documentation in other ways. I mention it only as a last resort in case other options aren't available.

As long as you can validate your homeschool 4.0 with good external documentation, feel free to grant it. On the flip side, don't be afraid to give lower grades if they truly reflect your student's performance. Honesty and internal consistency are key.

Socialization

So much has been written about this subject that I am hesitant to say much more about it here. Suffice it to say that homeschoolers have the advantage in socialization since they spend their childhood socializing across a broad spectrum of ages, classes, and cultures. They are not limited to the narrow socialization by age and status that you find in a typical American high school. Consequently, when they are called on to interact with adults in the college admission process, they often feel right at home.

Socialization was, in fact, the deciding character feature that brought my boys home with two full-tuition college scholarships. Since all 108 kids who were invited to the full day scholarship competition had great grades and high test scores, the admissions official told us they looked at social skills as the deciding criteria. How well did these young scholars interact with one another, the faculty, and the staff on campus when they thought no one was looking? Irony of ironies, my homeschoolers took two of the ten scholarships awarded based on socialization!

Character

Closely related to socialization is character. How well have your family values been absorbed by your kids? I have learned that character development is in direct proportion to the time spent with your kids. The quality time argument is a crock!

What truly matters is face time, which can be collected by the bushel when you are teaching your kids for four to six hours a day at home. The reason you don't hear about the negative effects of peer pressure in homeschool families is because the peers are typically siblings, who are all being nurtured by the same loving set of parents.

During the college admission process, character comes through best in the application essays. Encourage your teen to write about experiences that highlight their character. Brainstorm with them about the ways they have given themselves away to others during their childhood and adolescence. Did they come with you when you volunteered at church or in the community? If so, what did they learn? Did they ever visit shut-ins with you? How did this affect them? Character is a trait which is caught, rather than taught, so make sure your student can formulate these lessons into stories.

Self-motivation

This one is my favorite because of the delightful serendipity involved. I mean, who would have guessed that my unwillingness and/or inability to re-educate myself on higher level high school math and science would help, rather than hurt, my children? When has my laziness *ever* turned out so well? In this case it did. My kids had to learn the material, and since Lee and I felt incapable of teaching it, they had to make do themselves. And they did. With a little money thrown at the problem (buying a good curriculum and video tutorials), my boys basically taught themselves calculus and physics. The results were twofold. First, they learned how to self-teach. Second, they experienced the satisfaction associated with doing it themselves.

Lee and I noticed that the more we neglected teaching, the better our boys learned! Why? Because they knew they had no one to count on but themselves, and they had to get it done if they wanted any summer vacation at all!

Help your student reflect on the benefits of academic self-reliance, and communicate this on their application essays. They might be a bit skeptical at first, but I'm sure with a bit of effort, you can successfully make the case that your laziness was all part of the master plan.

Incidentally, if you encourage self-reliance, you are doing your teen a favor that will pay dividends when they go to college. Ironically, a favorite expression university professors share with their freshman population is, "I am not your parent." This is supposed to press the point that no one will baby the students to ensure they complete their work. But our boys discovered that their professors were like their parents (only much smarter). They already knew how to learn on their own, so they started college with a tremendous advantage over their spoon-fed peers.

Leadership

If you do well in the other four areas (academics, socialization, character, and self-motivation), leadership skills often emerge naturally. To be a leader, one must first *want* to be a leader. Often, the first step in wanting to be a leader is to lead successfully. You might consider this a bit of a Catch-22, but recognize that by promoting healthy attitudes about academics, socialization, character, and self-motivation, you are providing your student with this critical first leadership experience—that is, leading themselves.

Surprisingly, this works regardless of your student's personality type. My first-born was always shy and demure. As a baby, we didn't hear a peep from him for what seemed to be months. Probably because he didn't want to be a bother. My youngest, however, was born loudly demanding his rights! If he could have got his hands on a knife, I'm convinced he would have cut the cord himself. You might think leadership would be reserved for my youngest. The truth is, however, that both of my boys are leaders—in their own way. The youngest expressed a desire to lead for a living as a politician. The oldest led in each situation he found himself (the classroom, on projects, with his chess students). One leads loudly, one leads quietly.

When dealing with college applications, it is easy for extroverted teens to highlight leadership skills. Identifying leadership in the quiet teen is a bit more of a challenge. The quiet ones may not recognize their leadership at all. In such cases, you may need to gently point it out to them. But whether or not they see it in themselves, it is often recognized by outsiders. By the time my youngest, Alex, applied for college, he had amassed quite an impressive resume of leadership positions. But my eldest, Kevin, demonstrated his areas of quiet leadership during the full-tuition scholarship competition, and also came away with the big prize.

Social Dancing

My younger son became a big fan of English Country dancing. As opposed to what passes as "normal" teen dancing, English Country is a delightfully social dance style. The entire room must be in tune for the dance to succeed.

Similarly, college preparation is a social dance for the whole family. Mom and Dad play a secondary, yet critical role in developing the "dance skills" that will get their teens noticed by colleges. They are the "callers" in the English Country dance. Parents set the patterns and demonstrate how to do them properly.

There is much talk about the emergence of "helicopter parents." These are parents who throw their full influence and attention to the task of college admission. I liken these "helicopter parents," however, to the ones that do emergency airlifts. The patient (student) is in critical condition already, so Mom and Dad feel compelled to rescue them. Homeschool parents don't have to be in this position, however. They have the time to develop their kids in a natural and healthy way. No emergency intervention is required, because their kids have grown up in nurturing and loving environments, and can now step into the world with confidence.

Blue Chip Teens

There will always be a Bull Market for teens. The world eagerly awaits the next generation of leaders to emerge. When they do, I promise they will get noticed. Parents, you don't have to bang a gong to draw attention to your kids. Let their character, words, and actions speak for themselves. In a generation filled with the human equivalent of junk bonds, colleges are desperate to find and reward the blue chips. For increasingly more colleges, homeschool teens have proven to be a solid investment.

Matt Binz, Mr. HomeScholar

Appendix 1

Needed: Homeschool Mom Decoder

Men and women are gender aliens. Men are from Mars and women are from Venus. Pink talking and blue talking collide in waves of purplish conversations. How can we possibly cope when the two genders are so different? It's important, though, because our children count on us to communicate effectively. We have to talk about important things, such as education, family, and values, when it seems like we hardly speak the same language.

If only there was some sort of secret decoder ring that came in our cereal boxes...

We need some help so we can understand one another! Can't we all just get along?

Lee's Perspective

I talk a lot about translating our normal, natural homeschool into words and numbers colleges understand: grades, credits, and transcripts. But long before we make transcripts, other communication issues come into play. We have to translate our normal, natural homeschool frustrations into words and phrases our *husbands* can understand. Some might say it's even more challenging than converting a homeschool into educational-eze.

Here is my perspective. Men can be so hard to understand. They make everything so ... what's the word ... *logical*! But my husband claims that I am hard to understand! After all, he says I could simply start by saying what I mean in the first place. Ha! If only it were that easy! So I asked my husband, Matt, to explain.

Matt's Perspective

Never was this Venus/Mars thing more apparent than when we homeschooled. There seemed to be so many ... oh, what's the word ... *feelings* about everything related to the kids, their education and, surprisingly often, my parents. Most of these feelings were cleverly hidden under an enormous pile of ... oh, what's the word ... *words*! The flood of feelings and words that often greeted me after a long day at work could exceed a teenager's ability to text! Often, I would come to full understanding through a painful period of trial and error, using my prodigious communication skills and through the careful employment of strategic clarifying questions such as "Huh?" and "What??"

I captured some of these hard won lessons in a notebook to remind myself that some of the more common expressions Lee uttered did not always mean what they appeared to mean. Upon careful reflection and through the clarity that only weeping can bring, I was able to translate many of these comments and declarations into their true meaning.

It is in the spirit of love, service, and above all, pity for my fellow homeschool dads, that I share this battle-tested wisdom in the form of this "homeschool mom decoder." If I can save one dad from one night spent on the couch, my job is done.

And Back to Lee

As a public service, Matt and I are providing this Homeschool Mom Secret Decoder, below. Please share it with your spouse and friends for grins!

FROM THE DESK OF MR. HOMESCHOLAR COMES THE...

Homeschool Mom
Secret Decoder

When your wife says...	What she means is...	What she doesn't mean...
THE KIDS WERE AWFUL TODAY.	THE KIDS WERE AWFUL TODAY.	I WANT TO QUIT HOMESCHOOLING.
THIS PLACE IS A PIGSTY.	GET YOUR REAR IN HERE AND HELP WITH THE DISHES.	CAN I GET YOU A BEER, SWEETHEART?
JOHN ISN'T UNDERSTANDING HIS MATH LESSON.	HELP. JOHN. NOW.	JOHN TAKES AFTER YOUR MOTHER.
SUZY AND HER BEST FRIEND HAD A FIGHT TODAY.	GIRLS' EMOTIONS CAN BE SO HARD TO DEAL WITH.	WOMEN... CAN'T LIVE WITH 'EM...
THE DOG THREW UP ON THE CARPET.	PLEASE CLEAN THE CARPET.	HONEY, COULD YOU BRING ME A SPOON?
I FEEL LIKE A TOTAL FAILURE.	I FEEL LIKE A TOTAL FAILURE... HOLD ME...	HOLD ME,... TONIGHT'S THE NIGHT.
HOMESCHOOLING IS HARD.	COULD YOU PLEASE HOLD DOWN THE FORT WHILE I TAKE A BATH?	PUBLIC SCHOOL IS THE ONLY OPTION.

I QUIT.	TAG, YOU'RE IT!	PLEASE SUGGEST AN ALTERNATIVE CAREER I COULD PURSUE OUTSIDE THE HOME.
I CAN'T TAKE IT ANYMORE...	TRIPLE GRANDE CARAMEL MACCHIATO, NOT TOO HOT, EXTRA FOAM.	COULD YOU PLEASE EXPLAIN HOW I'M NOT BEING RATIONAL RIGHT NOW?
MY CHILDREN ARE HORRIBLE.	YOUR CHILDREN ARE HORRIBLE.	COULD YOU PLEASE GO YELL AND MAKE THE CHILDREN AND ME CRY.
I HATE HOMESCHOOLING.	TURN OFF THE TV AND LISTEN TO ME. I HAVE FEELINGS THAT WILL NOT BE DENIED.	HOMESCHOOLING WAS THE BIGGEST MISTAKE OF MY LIFE.
I CAN'T DO THIS ANYMORE.	I FEEL OVERWHELMED BY MY RESPONSIBILITIES. HELP ME!	PLEASE IGNORE ME. I'M JUST BEING AN EMOTIONAL WOMAN.
CAN YOU HELP ME DECIDE WHICH ROUTE TO GO IN THIS MATTER?	I WANT TO BOUNCE SOME IDEAS OFF YOU, IF YOU COULD SPARE A MINUTE, I VALUE YOUR INPUT.	YOU NEED TO TAKE A VACATION DAY AND FIGURE THIS OUT NOW!
I MISS FEELING SUCCESSFUL.	IT WOULD BE NICE TO GET FEEDBACK THAT HOMESCHOOLING IS THE RIGHT CHOICE.	MY OLD JOB WAS MORE IMPORTANT, AND MY OLD LIFE WAS BETTER.
THERE IS A GREAT HOMESCHOOL CONFERENCE GOING ON NEXT WEEKEND ...	DON'T MAKE ANY PLANS. YOU ARE BABYSITTING.	PLEASE TELL ME IF YOU THINK I SHOULD GO OR NOT.
I CAN'T GET A SINGLE THING DONE!	PLEASE FOLD SOME LAUNDRY.	PLEASE CALL UP YOUR MOTHER TO COME HELP ME OUT A BIT.

Alternative Perspectives

Guess what? Not every mom is the stay at home parent. Some dads are the primary educators at home. There are wonderfully successful single parents as well. Their voices are so important and vital to the homeschool community.

Suzy says this decoder is helpful even for single parents. She was thankful for the reminders, because her inner-voice speaks the mom words, and she needed help translating her own thoughts into what she really means.

"These are great! As a now-single mom I need to be reminded that the emotional expressions that are going through my own head (what I say to myself!) really may not be exactly what I mean. Your 'what she means is' actually can be a help so that *I* can figure out what I really mean! May all of you married moms offer up a special prayer for your special, if sometimes bewildered, homeschool hero husbands!"

A homeschool dad felt slighted by the implication that moms are always the home educators.

"Wives of male lawyers are not called 'lawyer moms' so I'm not sure why husbands of homeschool moms are 'homeschool dads.' I AM a homeschool dad, in that I have been my daughter's primary teacher for 6 years. My wife works full time as a public school teacher. I appreciate that we are an extreme minority. Please appreciate that the label 'homeschool dad' has a radically different, and mostly unappreciated definition for those of us who do this job."

Rachel makes the comparison to professionals working outside the home as well.

"When I was first homeschooling and would get stressed out and try to talk through it with my husband, he would often reply that maybe we should just put the kids in school. I finally said, 'What would you say if you came home to me to tell me about your hard day and

I told you to quit your job? Because that is what you are doing to me. I don't want to quit my job, I just need to talk through the newness of the difficulties here, just like you do.'"

What a great point!

Many of our parental conversations may seem like a classic communication played out in sitcoms night after night on TV. These are the times that try men's souls.

These are the moments we will look back on and cherish as we remember our homeschooling years, giggling together.

Appendix 2

But What about Football?

Dear Confused Homeschool Dad,

I understand that nearing the end of this book you may still be left with some lingering questions, such as "Huh?" and "Who plugged the toilet this time?" In case the whole homeschool thing still leaves you a bit puzzled, allow me to break it down for you in a way you will surely understand.

Professional football players know their game is a metaphor for life. With each new football season, some of us die-hard fans might become so engrossed by what's happening on the field that we miss valuable lessons we can apply to our homeschooling.

Let's look at homeschooling through a gridiron lens, so you can become a professional success in your career as a homeschool dad. Each stage of the game yields valuable insights you can use. Check out this play-by-play to learn what you can about each stage of homeschooling high school.

Tailgate Party: Elementary School

Before the game even begins, fans start celebrating a win. The homeschool tailgate party is elementary school, when education is all about food, folks, and fun. Feed the love of learning, share true socialization with parents and friends, and add joy by making subjects more fun to learn. These lessons can be integrated into daily life, nurturing the budding intellect.

Pre-Game Warm-Up: Middle School

Before play begins, team members stretch their muscles. The warm-up for high school is middle school. Parents stretch themselves by learning about high school, and children stretch their academic abilities. It's the time to identify strengths and shore up weaknesses.

Communication is key to ensure all participants are on the same page. Parents must review the game plan to understand what is coming, so the team can play as if each game is a step toward the Super Bowl. Team players must know their opponents, such as chemistry, calculus, and economics. These opponents can be defeated with a solid game plan and plenty of practice, so the pre-game warm-up is essential for success.

First Quarter: Freshman Year

Kickoff is game time; it's no time to panic. For homeschool parents, freshman year is a time to calm nerves. You have practiced and prepared, and had a successful pre-season. Now is not the time to be freaked out or terrified.

Someone has to score first, and sadly, it may not be you. If you give up a touchdown or two, don't quit! Stick to your game plan, and cover the core classes. You'll be prepared for anything, no matter the score at the end of the first quarter.

Second Quarter: Sophomore Year

Coaches know getting on the scoreboard during the first half is critical. Homeschool parents should get a good start with their sophomore. Add foreign language, fine art, P.E., and electives, so you can score early with high school credits. Have your child take the PSAT for fun and enroll in college prep classes to earn more points toward college admission and scholarships.

Pro teams adapt and make substitutions during the game. Great homeschool parents do the same, changing curriculum and scheduling substitutions to adapt when challenges occur. It's important to outscore your opponent this quarter, so you can start the second half with a lead.

Half Time: Summer before Junior Year

During half time, football coaches continue to work. They have learned new information about their opponents, and can regroup to make adjustments for the second half. Without looking back, they keep their eyes forward to see how they can win.

Homeschool parents are their children's best coaches when they look ahead to junior year to develop a plan. Talk about the coming second half, make a plan, and make course corrections. Parents can get new information about their opponents by learning more about college admission and scholarships.

Third Quarter: Junior Year

To win a football game, it helps to gain or keep the lead in the third quarter. It's difficult to come from behind in the fourth, and impossible to win if you're not on the scoreboard! For homeschoolers, the third quarter is junior year—the key to success. Run up the score during 11th grade in five big ways. Take the PSAT, attend a college fair, take the SAT or ACT, visit college campuses, and make some college choices. Each score gets you one step closer to victory.

Fourth Quarter: Senior Year

Keep the score in your favor. Avoid a last minute Hail Mary play; it rarely works, and it gives control to your opponent. Homeschoolers should start senior year strong, and not let go of their lead.

This quarter, get on the scoreboard in three big ways. Apply to at least four colleges early in the fall, personalize college applications with self-reflective essays, and complete the FAFSA for maximum scholarships. Glide through the quarter, maintaining your lead so you can win the college admission game.

Super Celebration: Spring of Senior Year

From the first Sunday game to the Super Bowl, every win is a celebration. Homeschoolers celebrate with unique graduations for their seniors. Plan a graduation party, ticker-tape parade optional. Give a meaningful trophy—the high school diploma and transcript. Choose your MVP—the best college for your child.

It's All about Teamwork

A win worth celebrating comes from teamwork. For homeschool parents and students, this means true education represented by comprehensive homeschool records combined with helpful test scores. Winning teams value the fundamentals of a college prep education. Super Bowl teams maximize the special abilities of their franchise players. In the same way, homeschool parents can maximize the fun factor in education, embracing their children's passions with delight directed learning on the homeschool transcript.

Winning throughout an entire football season takes skill but also luck, because of challenging schedules and possible injuries. But good teams plan ahead for these problems. As the great Vince Lombardi said, "Luck is where preparation meets opportunity."

Great homeschool parents plan ahead for problems, too. Be consistent from the beginning, so you never fall behind. Be prepared for anything by planning a college prep education that maximizes learning, because teenagers change their minds. Your star player will be prepared for anything this way—from college to career!

See below for a handy tear out page you can fold and keep in your wallet for the next 18 years.

HOME FIELD ADVANTAGE
Better Homeschooling through Football

Tailgate Party = Elementary School
- Learn to love learning
- True socialization

Pre-game Warmup = Middle School
- Learn about high school
- Stretch abilities, shore up weaknesses

1st Quarter = Freshman Year
- Cover the core classes
- Do not panic

2nd Quarter = Sophomore Year
- Add foreign language and electives
- Take the PSAT for fun

3rd Quarter = Junior Year
- Take the PSAT, and SAT or ACT
- Attend a college fair and visit colleges

4th Quarter = Senior Year
- Apply to 4-8 colleges
- Write essays, complete the FAFSA

Super Bowl Celebration = Graduation!
- Choose a college, plan a party
- Provide a transcript and diploma

Winning Advice
- Provide a college prep education
- Create comprehensive homeschool records
- Arrange helpful college admission tests
- Include delight direct learning
- Always be prepared for college or career

www.TheHomeScholar.com • HomeScholar

Matt Binz, Mr. HomeScholar

Afterword

Who is Matt Binz and What Can He Do for Me?

Well ... truth be told, not much. He's only a working schmo who's happy he survived homeschooling with his marriage and family intact. Other than this book ... that's it.

His wife, however, is chock-full of yummy homeschooling goodness, and could be a great help to you and your family during the homeschool high school years.

Number one best-selling homeschool author, Lee Binz is The HomeScholar. Her mission is "helping parents homeschool high school." Lee and her husband, Matt, homeschooled their two boys, Kevin and Alex, from elementary through high school.

Upon graduation, both boys received four-year, full tuition scholarships from their first choice university. This enables Lee to pursue her dream job - helping parents homeschool their children through high school.

On The HomeScholar website, you will find great products for creating homeschool transcripts and comprehensive records to help you amaze and impress colleges.

Find out why Andrew Pudewa, Director of the Institute for Excellence in Writing says: "Lee Binz knows how to navigate this often confusing and frustrating labyrinth better than anyone."

You can find Lee online at:

HomeHighSchoolHelp.com

If this book has been helpful, could you please take a minute to write us a quick review on Amazon?

Thank you!

Testimonials

A Great Investment

"This past fall I participated in one of your free webinars and purchased some of your material related to transcripts and college applications. We're hearing back from colleges now with acceptances, invitations to honors programs and merit scholarships. Thank you so much for your guidance, advice and encouragement. Your material was a great investment!"

~ Marilyn in California

A Confidence Booster

"Just wanted to shoot you a note to say THANK YOU. My daughter applied online to the university of her first choice. She had to send in a hard copy of her transcript. We sent that in, but in addition and thanks to your guidance, we also sent in a cover letter followed by her comprehensive record. Your assistance via the phone was invaluable and was a great confidence booster as we embarked on this journey.

Thanks again!"

~ Chrystal in Georgia

For more information about the **Gold Care Club**, go to:

GoldCareClub.com

Also From The HomeScholar ...

- The HomeScholar Guide to College Admission and Scholarships: Homeschool Secrets to Getting Ready, Getting In and Getting Paid (Book and Kindle Book)
- Setting the Records Straight—How to Craft Homeschool Transcripts and Course Descriptions for College Admission and Scholarships (Book and Kindle Book)
- TechnoLogic: How to Set Logical Technology Boundaries and Stop the Zombie Apocalypse
- Finding the Faith to Homeschool High School
- The Easy Truth About Homeschool Transcripts (Kindle Book)

- Parent Training A la Carte (Online Training)
- Total Transcript Solution (Online Training, Tools and Templates)
- Comprehensive Record Solution (Online Training, Tools and Templates)
- Gold Care Club (Comprehensive Online Support and Training)
- Silver Training Club (Online Training)

The HomeScholar Coffee Break Books Released or Coming Soon on Kindle and Paperback:

- Delight Directed Learning: Guiding Your Homeschooler Toward Passionate Learning
- Creating Transcripts for Your Unique Child: Help Your Homeschool Graduate Stand Out from the Crowd
- Beyond Academics: Preparation for College and for Life
- Planning High School Courses: Charting the Course Toward High School Graduation
- Graduate Your Homeschooler in Style: Make Your Homeschool Graduation Memorable

- Keys to High School Success: Get Your Homeschool High School Started Right!
- Getting the Most Out of Your Homeschool This Summer: Learning just for the Fun of it!
- Finding a College: A Homeschooler's Guide to Finding a Perfect Fit
- College Scholarships for High School Credit: Learn and Earn With This Two-for-One Strategy!
- College Admission Policies Demystified: Understanding Homeschool Requirements for Getting In
- A Higher Calling: Homeschooling High School for Harried Husbands (by Matt Binz, Mr. HomeScholar)
- Gifted Education Strategies for Every Child: Homeschool Secrets for Success
- College Application Essays: A Primer for Parents
- Creating Homeschool Balance: Find Harmony Between Type A and Type Zzz...
- Homeschooling the Holidays: Sanity Saving Strategies and Gift Giving Ideas
- Your Goals this Year: A Year by Year Guide to Homeschooling High School

- Making the Grades: A Grouch-Free Guide to Homeschool Grading
- High School Testing: Knowledge That Saves Money
- Getting the BIG Scholarships: Learn Expert Secrets for Winning College Cash!
- Easy English for Simple Homeschooling: How to Teach, Assess and Document High School English
- Scheduling—The Secret to Homeschool Sanity: Plan You Way Back to Mental Health
- Junior Year is the Key to High School Success: How to Unlock the Gate to Graduation and Beyond
- Upper Echelon Education: How to Gain Admission to Elite Universities
- How to Homeschool College: Save Time, Reduce Stress and Eliminate Debt
- Homeschool Curriculum That's Effective and Fun: Avoid the Crummy Curriculum Hall of Shame!
- Comprehensive Homeschool Records: Put Your Best Foot Forward to Win College Admission and Scholarships
- Options After High School: Steps to Success for College or Career

- How to Homeschool 9th and 10th Grade: Simple Steps for Starting Strong!
- Senior Year Step-by-Step: Simple Instructions for Busy Homeschool Parents
- How to Homeschool Independently: Do-it-Yourself Secrets to Rekindle the Love of Learning
- High School Math The Easy Way: Simple Strategies for Homeschool Parents in Over Their Heads
- Homeschooling Middle School with Powerful Purpose: How to Successfully Navigate 6th through 8th Grade
- Simple Science for Homeschooling High School: Because Teaching Science isn't Rocket Science!

Would you like to be notified when we offer the next *Coffee Break Books* for FREE during our Kindle promotion days? If so, leave your name and email below and we will send you a reminder.

HomeHighSchoolHelp.com/ freekindlebook

Visit my Amazon Author Page!

amazon.com/author/leebinz

Made in the USA
Lexington, KY
03 December 2019